Basic **trek**

Basic trek

Venture into a world of enough

Edited by Dave Schrock-Shenk
Commissioned by Mennonite Central Committee

Herald
Press

Scottdale, Pennsylvania
Waterloo, Ontario

Library of Congress Cataloging-in-Publication Data

Basic trek: venture into a world of enough / edited by Dave Schrock-Shenk; commissioned by Mennonite Central Committee.
    p. cm.
  Includes bibliographical references.
  ISBN 0-8361-9215-X (alk. paper)
  1. Simplicity—Religious aspects—Mennonites—Meditations. I. Schrock-Shenk, Dave, 1955- II. Mennonite Central Committee.

BV4647.S48 B37 2002
241'.68—dc21

2002019664

The paper used in this publication is recycled and meets the minimum requirements of American National Standard for Information Sciences—Permanence of Paper for Printed Library Materials, ANSI Z39.48-1984.

Scripture is from the *New Revised Standard Version Bible*, copyright 1989 by the Division of Christian Education of the National Council of the Churches of Christ in the USA, and is used by permission, with all rights reserved.

BASIC TREK
Copyright © 2002 by Herald Press, Scottdale, Pa. 15683
   Published simultaneously in Canada by Herald Press,
   Waterloo, Ont. N2L 6H7. All rights reserved
Library of Congress Catalog Card Number: 2002019664
International Standard Book Number: 0-8361-9215-X
Printed in the United States of America
Book and cover design by Julie Kauffman

10 09 08 07 06 05 04 03 02 10 9 8 7 6 5 4 3 2 1

To order or request information, call 1-800-759-4447 (individuals); 1-800-245-7894 (trade). Website: www.mph.org

Consider the lilies . . .

Matthew 6:25-33

enough? what a concept! Our society seems to

say, "You need more. More is better. You are 'out of it' unless you have this . . . and this . . . and this." We often find ourselves wearily asking, "How much can I afford? Can I fit this one more activity into my busy schedule?" A pastor from the Philippines once observed, "The point of our Christian faith is not that we have less than we need, but that everyone has enough." A simple idea . . . enough for everyone. Enough food . . . enough clothes . . . enough recreation . . . enough time with family . . . enough quietness . . . enough time with God. But what is enough? *Basic Trek* invites us to explore that question. In thought. And in experience. Take this *Trek* with friends—a youth group, a dorm wing, friends from church, or *Trek* as a family. Friends are important, not to tell us how to think or live, but to share stories and encouragement along the trail.

the 28-day trek

A different theme is featured for each of the four weeks. The first week you will **awaken to the journey** to find enough joy, the second week you **step out** to explore enough simplicity, the third week you **lighten the pack** in your search for enough for me, and the fourth week you **stay the course** to discover enough for all.

Each day starts with a story and a Scripture passage followed by reflection questions to consider and actions to try. Also check out the key concepts and references in the appendix. All these invite us to live, reflect, and walk into a world of enough for all.

how to approach

When groups go swimming, some brave souls always jump in the water first, then call to those on shore, "Try it, you'll like it!" The stories and Scriptures in *Basic Trek* invite us to reflect on the question, "What is enough?" We are also invited to jump in and try living with enough. There are, of course, different ways of entering the water. **the plunge approach:** Some people like to jump in head first. Folks like that may want to study the "ecological footprints" and "global classes" in this booklet, then map out an "enough lifestyle" they will live with for four weeks. **the tiptoe approach:** Other people like to get wet in stages. First they dip their toes in the water, then their feet, then go in up to their knees, etc. Folks like that will likely focus on the suggested actions for each day of *Trek*. Some of these actions take only one day to complete, others take a week, and others might extend past the one month of *Trek*. Don't try to do every action—you'll drive yourself crazy! Choose the ones that are right for you. If the action for one day doesn't feel right, make up your own.

bracket your month. start by spending time together in a way that embodies enough. enthusiastic groups may want to spend a weekend at someone's house, sleeping on floors, preparing meals with local ingredients, studying the information in Trek, planning for the month, playing together, doing a small service project, and worshiping together. others may spend an evening or part of a day together. at the end of each week or the month reconvene to share your thoughts and plan for future steps.
happy trails!

ENOUGH JOY ENOUGH JOY ENOUGH JOY ENOUGH JOY ENOUGH JOY ENOUGH JOY ENOUG

week one

awaken
to the
journey

OY ENOUGH JOY ENOUGH JOY ENOUGH JOY ENOUGH JOY ENOUGH JOY ENOUGH JOY ENOUGH JOY

June 13, 2015

the meaning of life

*"I came that they may have life,
and have it abundantly."*
—from John 10:7-18

1

this week we look at the meaning of life. What were we created to do and be? Where do we want to go with our lives? How can we find our purpose and fulfill it? **North American culture** gives conflicting advice about how to maximize our enjoyment of life. Ads for the U.S. military say, "Be all that you can be, join the Army." Can we find fulfillment by learning to fight? A famous watch ad says, "You can never be too rich, or too thin." Do we find fulfillment by having a supermodel's body and an unlimited fortune? One beer commercial shows men fishing in a mountain lake with coolers of beer, then says, "It doesn't get any better than this." Does real fulfillment come in a can? **Jesus said he came** to bring us a full, abundant life. During this week we will reflect on what we think a fulfilled or abundant life is. Our understandings of what life is about grow out of our deepest beliefs. They reflect who we understand God to be, and how we think the world works. Sharing these beliefs with each other is not to decide who is "right" and who is "wrong." It involves learning from each other about the deepest mysteries of our existence.

—Dave Schrock-Shenk

**what was I
created to do
and be?**

AWAKEN TO THE JOURNEY

1. cook
2. organize
3. care for people
4. love my family
5. mow the yard
6. be dependable
7. plan events
8. take care of finances
9. show hospitality
10. juggle multiple tasks

A vision of the abundant life can seem very grand and sweeping— and very impersonal.

Each of us is created with a set of skills and interests.

We live a fulfilled life when we find out how we personally fit into the larger vision.

what Scripture passage, poem, story, song, or quotation sums up what I think life is about?

what images or pictures come to mind when I think of Jesus' statement that he came to bring us an "abundant life"?

list 10 things you can do very well.

poem in Greek

Ephesians 2:10 For we are God's workmanship, created in Christ Jesus to do good works, which God prepared in advance for us to do.

Everyone having enough of the basic necessaties for life (water, food, shelter, clothing, self respect). No small group of people hoarding which causes others not to have enough

ent to Costco & Meijer today. So many things to tempt me. Did buy lots of different snacks to get more protein in my diet.

missing almost everything

"I have suffered the loss of all things . . .
that I may gain Christ . . ."
—from Philippians 3:7-16

2

how am I affected by the options that surround me?

"the secret of the spiritual life** is the willingness to miss almost everything" *(author unknown)*. **as a North American** I've learned to equate freedom with options. A nearby store advertises 135 kinds of cereals. But too many options paralyze me! How can I "check out all the options" when there are so many? **in my 20s** I thought I could do everything; work long term for the church, marry, raise a family, dedicate myself to others, live a "normal" life. When I turned 35, I realized abruptly that before long I would no longer have the option of bearing children. Choices have consequences. **yet I regret** none of my life choices. Dedicating myself to people who are poor means some options are no longer available. Yet I feel more free, since I am not sidetracked by exploring every door I encounter. "Keeping my options open" is possible only at the expense of long-term commitment and direction for my life. **following Jesus** means accepting that the way is narrow. Walking faithfully doesn't offer the lure of endless options. But the boundaries provided by committing myself to the narrow way provide the framework I need so my energy can flow with purpose and direction. **being willing** to "miss almost everything" enables me to live my unique, spiritual calling fully and deeply.
—*Susan Classen*

AWAKEN TO THE JOURNEY

I would like to truthfully say that God's important above all else in my life, but I tend to put whatever I feel is important in my life at the moment ahead of everything else. Sometimes it is my family and soon it may be working as a pastor. However, the majority of the time I try to make sure I spend time with God throughout my day.

It is one thing to understand something we can see or touch. It is another thing to have a relationship with God, whom we cannot see or touch.

We cannot use someone else's standards to judge our relationship with God. Asking ourselves honest questions will increase our self-awareness.

In a limited lifetime, we cannot do everything. Choosing to do one thing often means we cannot do something else. Fulfillment comes when our fundamental choices reflect our fundamental values.

can I honestly say, "God is important above all else in my life"?

what life choices have I made that reflect my relationship with God? *going to seminary and becoming a pastor at my age*

spend 15 minutes today with God. this time could be spent praying, reflecting as you take a walk, reading the Bible, or journaling. consider making time with God part of each day.

Took Eric to Kohls today to shop for Father's day. Bought Aaron a really cool tie. I know he has plenty of ties bought just because I like to give people things I wanted him to have one.

6/15/16

taxing wildflowers

*"The pastures of the wilderness overflow,
the hills gird themselves with joy . . ."
—from Psalm 65*

3

When I do my taxes, I discover my government defines my family as poor. Here's how poor we are. **my five-year-old** announces, "A hepatica is blooming on the hill!" Last year we transplanted a few native wildflowers onto our hill. (What is the value of one hepatica on my tax form?) **my husband** badly strained his back several years ago—fairly catastrophic for a market gardener. Our friends helped out: One eight-year-old pulled every buttonweed out of our greenbeans. (What's the dollar amount put on friendship?) **as a mother** of young children, finding quiet time is not easy. My best prayer time is in the morning while I milk the goats. (Dear tax collector: May I deduct the cost of 30 minutes per day with the Great Consultant as a farm expense?) **in the midst** of my work I am getting in touch with my God. **my husband and I** could earn more money in other professions. But would we have time for wildflower projects that delight our son? Could we and our neighbors help each other? Would I make space in my life for prayer if we got rid of the goats that are not "economically viable"? I will continue to measure my wealth by standards other than "adjusted gross income." I am happy to be so richly poor.

—*Ellen L. Davis-Zehr*

what standards do I use to evaluate my choices in life?

AWAKEN TO THE JOURNEY

Today was a "spoil Debbie" day. I had a pedicure, manicure, and a massage and took a friend to lunch. While some people would deem these as "extremely frivolous," I look at them as being forms of "self-preservation." Going to the massage therapist helps my back from hurting and relaxes me from the tension I've been experiencing. I also look at it as a way to support others in their jobs/careers.

Each of us makes choices about how to spend our lives. As we live out those choices, other people let us know in many ways whether they think our choices are valid or important.

Ultimately we need to decide if we feel good about those choices, based on the values and commitments that led us to make the choices in the first place.

are my core values reflected in my lifestyle?

are my core values or push me away from being true to what I believe?

I really don't know who this would be.

do my closest friends support my values

think about the person whose lifestyle you find most challenging. invite that person to a meal. talk together about your dreams and values.

Not everything we do is self-centered. Eric and I are quite generous with our income by today's standards.

I think my close friends do not oppose what I do. Don't remember any of them speaking against and often applaud us for the ways we support the church.

I do not just want to give money to organizations without knowing what they do with it

6/16/15

i've seen the pygmies dance . . .

"The mountains and the hills before you shall burst into song . . ."
—from Isaiah 55:6-13

i **have been** surprised by life.

What an amazing amount of experiences I've had in the past forty years.

Some good . . . and some bad . . .

I've seen the pygmies dance.

I swam in the Indian Ocean.

I gathered seashells on Zanzibar Island.

I've seen the whirling dervishes in Khartoum.

And a riot in the middle of Kampala.

I've smelled incense from sandalwood, frankincense, and myrrh.

And open sewers, burning trash, rotting flesh,

drying fish, and camel dung.

I've awakened to the Muslim call to prayer.

I heard the explosion of a land mine.

And gunshots fired in celebration, in fear,

in anger, and in rebellion.

what unexpected joy has life brought me?
An AK 47 was aimed at me as thieves stole our car.

I know there is much in life that I have not experienced,

nor have I lived as fully as I was capable.

I am surprised that those regrets aren't the focus of my life.

AWAKEN TO THE JOURNEY

- being Eric's wife and Aaron and Sarah's mother
- helping/serving others
- knowing that I have a difference in someone's life

Now I am catching glimpses of my life at fifty years, at sixty years
       and at eighty years.
What a joy to discover that I may have half of my life to live.
Forty more years of choices, of experiences and of people.
Forty more years with a man I love.
And forty more years of walking, loving, and living with my God.
I am surprised.
—*Pam Ferguson*

what experiences give me my deepest joy?

are there ways I could earn a living while serving others?

write a poem or create a photo collage that captures the high points of your life so far.

It's been said God calls us to that place "where our deep gladness and the world's deep hunger meet."

The meditation writer talks about experiences of danger, and of being with people in need. Yet her poem says this life has been good. She did not need to choose between having a fulfilled life and working for others.

Many people work at jobs they find unexciting because they have no option. Others choose work that does not express their deepest values because it pays well.

Being able to find work that provides for our own needs while serving others sometimes depends on how we define our needs.

I will be doing that as of 7/1 ☺

A photo collage would include picture from wedding on our shelf in our bedroom, picture of kids at VBS, picture from AMBS graduation, picture of Trinity, picture of our house and flowers pictures from various trips we've taken

fishy assumptions

*"One's life does not consist
in the abundance of possessions."
—from Luke 12:13-34*

5

Sometimes I am tempted to think if I could accumulate a sufficient nest egg, I could relax and have time for what I consider the important things in life: quality time with friends and family, or service with folks who have experienced hard times.

I have an unsettling feeling some fallacy lies hidden in this logic, that I am missing some liberating paradox of biblical proportions. A story of Anthony de Mello, the priest from India, reminds me of that paradox.

The rich industrialist from the North was horrified to find the Southern fisherman lying leisurely beside his boat.

"Why aren't you fishing?" asked the industrialist.

"Because I have caught enough fish for the day," said the fisherman.

"Why don't you catch some more?"

"What would I do with it?"

what is a good balance of "deferred gratification" and "taking no thought for tomorrow"?

"You could earn more money," was the reply. "With that you could fix a motor to your boat, go into deeper waters and catch more fish. Then you would make enough to buy nylon nets. These would bring you more fish and more money. Soon you would have enough money to own two boats . . . maybe even a fleet of boats. Then you would be a rich man like me."

"What would I do then?"

"Then you could really enjoy life."

"What do you think I am doing right now?"

—Earl Martin

22

Spend an evening with one of your parents, a grandparent, or other friend who has retired. Invite them to talk about the choices they made about how to spend their lives. What choices have brought them the most joy? What do they wish they had done more of?

will the amount of things I own continue to grow throughout my life, or will I eventually say, "that's enough"?

I want to have this discussion with Eric. this is not something I can do on my own

spend fifteen minutes today with God. this time could be spent praying, reflecting as you take a walk, reading the Bible, or journaling. consider making time with God part of each day.

what I can do what I really want to do?

I am going to be doing what I really want to do as of 7/1

how much do I need to accumulate before I can do what I really want to do?

what am I doing now to enjoy life?

Waiting to finish school so I can have time to enjoy life with Eric. For now travel + playing games

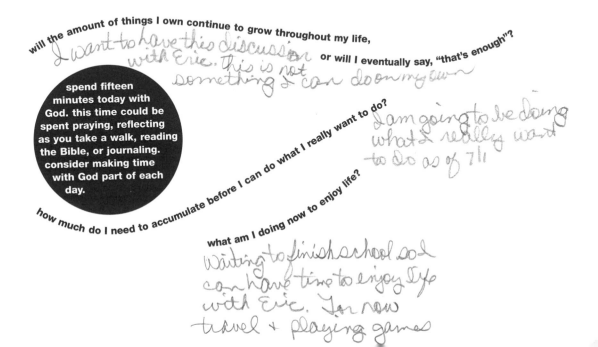

6/18/15

freedom from pretense

"Everyone . . . had all things in common. . . .
They . . . ate their food with glad and generous hearts."
—from Acts 2:43-47

6

One thing I appreciate about the Lao people I have known is their lack of pretense. No doubt some of this is cultural. It is also related to poverty. Material hardship means people must share with each other. This encourages freedom to be oneself, without trying to maintain an image of self-sufficiency. **this was especially** evident to me during one lengthy trip to several rural Lao provinces. We slept in small rooms with open windows and doors. The daily rhythms of life—cooking, bathing, washing clothes, and visiting—happened outdoors in shared spaces. **our room** was not the private sanctuary it is in the West. Lao colleagues would poke their heads in the window to greet us. With time we learned to enjoy this closeness and informality. **when we arrived** in a large town and stayed in a hotel with individual, air-conditioned rooms and private baths, I felt cut off from the colleagues with whom I had shared the past weeks. Gone were the open windows and the need to sit together on the porch for a breath of fresh air. Gone was the sense of needing each other. **I often ponder** how our wealth affects us. While I enjoy the comfort of my home, have I given up the freedom to feel at home with others? While I cherish my independence, have I given up the freedom to admit my needs to others?
—Linda Gehman Peachey

do I use the things I own to build walls or bridges between myself and others?

When human beings enter nature, they are entering God's space.

When human beings build a house, they enclose part of nature, and create their own space. Their enclosures protect them from the elements. Making "our own space" is part of being human.

The challenge is to create space that is inviting to others while offering us the protection from the elements and some degree of privacy, which we all need.

The fact that Eric and I have our own computers tell me that we value private space.

what messages do I receive about the need or desirability of "having my own space"?

who gives me those messages?

Eric is closest + most obvious. The kids since they are older also send me that message

if a fire destroyed my place who would I ask to give me emergency housing?

Keith + Barb, even though we have Eric's family in the area

talk with your Trek group about things people in the group are planning to buy in the next six months. select something to buy and use in common.

—not in a Trek group

one thing needed

"He entered a certain village,
where a woman named Martha welcomed him into her home . . ."
—from Luke 10:38-42

7

When I came to the town called Belo Jardim, Doña Josefa, a widow, opened her home to me. Doña Josefa, seventy, was my neighbor for two years. At any hour of the day I was welcome to visit her, and more than likely would find other women in her living room, also drawn by her wisdom and humor. She was pleased to lay aside her tasks and focus on what was most important to her—people. She showed no concern for preparing for visitors; she knew her presence was most important. "Mary . . . sat at the Lord's feet and listened. . . . But Martha was distracted by her many tasks. . . ." **I had always** called ahead. Invited people far in advance. Cleaned the house. Worried about whether I had prepared enough food. **Doña Josefa often called** me her daughter. I wonder how much I have learned from this new mother of mine. Can it be that I have learned a most important lesson? That my frantic preparations distract me? That my guests will feel most welcome when I lay aside my tasks and focus on them? "The Lord answered . . . you are worried and distracted by many things; there is need of only one thing . . ."

—*Sally Jacober*

what is the finest gift I can offer a visitor who comes into my life?

BASIC TREK

AWAKEN TO THE JOURNEY

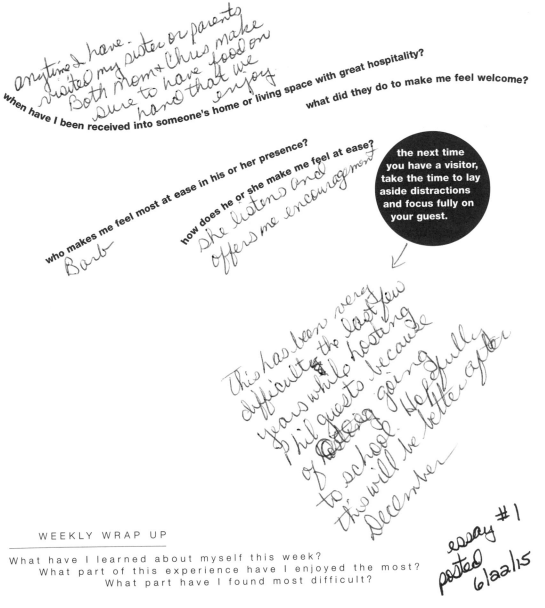

when have I been received into someone's home or living space with great hospitality?

anytime I have. visited my sister or parents. Both mom + Chris make sure to have food on hand that we enjoy.

what did they do to make me feel welcome?

who makes me feel most at ease in his or her presence?

Barb

how does he or she make me feel at ease?

She listens and offers me encouragement

the next time you have a visitor, take the time to lay aside distractions and focus fully on your guest.

This has been very difficult the last few years while hosting Phil guests because of ... going to school. Hopefully this will be better after December

WEEKLY WRAP UP

What have I learned about myself this week?
What part of this experience have I enjoyed the most?
What part have I found most difficult?

essay #1 posted 6/22/15

ENOUGH SIMPLICITY ENOUGH SIMPLICITY ENOUGH SIMPLICITY ENOUGH SIMPLICITY

step out

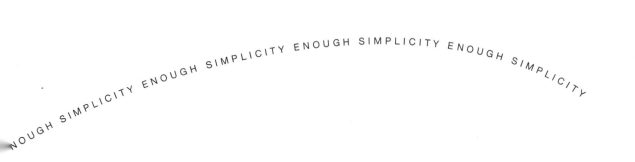

ENOUGH SIMPLICITY ENOUGH SIMPLICITY ENOUGH SIMPLICITY ENOUGH SIMPLICITY

the terror of sufficiency

"I do not understand my own actions.
For I do not do what I want, but I do the very thing I hate."
—from Romans 7:14-25

8

the people in the small Mexican town we visited were materially poor by any standard. Yet they laughed, joked, and worked together. They gathered at church to worship, and at the school to talk and play. **"life is good** here," I thought, "Even without many of the things I have." **then I wondered,** "What gives my life meaning?" I thought first of Caleb, my son. Then of special times with Carolyn and my intentional community, the annual flower planting on our block, and good times at work and at church. **I did not think** of my house, car, TV, videocassette recorder, or any other "thing." **my internal conversation** continued. "You believe the gap between rich and poor violates God's will. You believe using so many 'things' is ruining the earth. If family and friends give your life meaning, why not sell your car and move into a smaller house? You'll have enough, and you'll be living more in line with your beliefs." **"sell my car!"** A negative image of riding a bus, feeling trapped and dependent flooded me. "And how can I sell my house? How could we make do with less space?" **then I stopped,** stunned by my own response. Even though my experience and beliefs told me I could have a fulfilled life with fewer things, my guts wrenched when I thought about doing with less. **"why is the thought** of enough so daunting?" I wondered. "How can I break the stranglehold my things have on me and move toward the lifestyle my beliefs suggest?"
—*Dave Schrock-Shenk*

what gives my life meaning?

"Things" can sustain us, allow us to express our creativity and help strengthen relationships. Things can also distract us from doing what we want with our lives.

Our interaction with material things can give them a "life of their own." Understanding that relationship can be critical to finding our deepest joy and meaning in life.

what do I own that is not necessary for the activities I find most meaningful?

what would I do with my free time if I only had to spend half as much time working?

many of the knicknacks sitting around — including the piano, china, basement furniture. All of these things were used at various times in my life.

travel, read, volunteer

the Ecological Footprint section in the appendix (p 77) says most North Americans would need to shrink their Ecological Footprint by two-thirds to reach the global average. major items in those calculations include transportation, food, and housing. figure how much you or your household spends each year on these three items. figure how much you would save if your expenses for these items were reduced by two-thirds.

6/21/15

give us this day

*"Has not God chosen the poor in the world . . .
to be heirs of the kingdom?"*
—from James 2:1-7

teacher, can I borrow five baht?" **I looked into** the sweat-streaked face of Piak, one of my twelve-year-old students, who had just asked for about twenty cents U.S. He had just come from Bangkok's Garbage Mountain, where he makes his living sorting through the garbage, finding glass, tin, paper and plastic to resell. **"why do you** need five baht? Planning to go gamble with your friends?" I joked. **"no, teacher,"** he answered, "Yesterday I was sick so I only made ten baht instead of my usual fifteen baht. Now I am short five baht and cannot buy medicine for my grandmother." **Piak then told me** his parents had recently abandoned him, his sister and grandmother. Each day after morning classes, he would rush to the mountain to work until nightfall. With ten of the fifteen baht he earned, he would buy food for himself, his sister and his grandmother. His remaining five baht went for medicine for his grandmother's persistent cough. **I was angry** at myself for having joked about gambling. Perhaps it reflected the prejudice many of us have that the poor are poor because they are lazy and waste their money. I reached into my pocket and pulled out 100 baht. **"here, take this,"** I said. "Tonight buy yourself a little extra food." **"no, teacher.** I only want five baht. Tomorrow I will skip school and work extra hard. I can pay you back in the evening," he said. **the five-baht coin** seemed like precious gold as I handed it to him. He smiled and said, "Thank you, teacher. Tomorrow I will pay you back, I promise." **as I watched** him

what lesson did the school director learn from Piak?

BASIC TREK

trudge away, tears ran down my face. How much Piak could teach the world if it would only listen.

—*As told to Max Ediger by the Soi On Nhut primary school director*

Life has a material base. The "first set" of things we need to survive—food, clothing, and shelter—are absolutely essential.

In Matthew 6 Jesus told his disciples God knows we need these things, that we can pray to God for these things, and that God will provide them for us.

Few of us in North America work as hard as Piak. Yet almost anyone with a job earns more than Piak, because the global economic system "magnifies" our earning power far beyond others.

If those of us with magnified earning power would learn to be satisfied with enough, we would not only be able to share more with people like Piak, we would be able to live less frantic, stressful lives.

spend the evening star-gazing. invite a "veteran star gazer" to join you and help identify the basic constellations. end your evening with a prayer for all who watch these stars at night, and who pray to the Creator of the universe for daily bread.

does the way Piak provides for his family seem like the fulfillment of God's promise in Matthew 6?
he gets what they need each day but school would be better if he could just go to school

do I work more hours each week than I would like to?
not at this time - will be interesting to see how I feel after finishing school and only have

if so, what would need to happen for me to be able to work less?
I will need to be careful to balance family time + work time

joy is not in things, it is in us

"Why do you spend your money for that which is not bread,
and your labor for that which does not satisfy?"
—from Isaiah 55:1-5

10

ast year on Mother's Day, Laura, my eleven-year-old daughter, outlined what she likes about me: (1) you make great food! (2) you read great stories! (3) you take me shopping! **each item involves** an investment of time rather than money. **when I take** my children's preferences into account, they don't pick at what I cook. They are happy with pancakes and scrambled eggs, spaghetti and pizza, and plain, good bread. **I was amazed** that my bookworm daughter listed the stories I read. She can easily read books for herself. But when we read together, we cuddle on the bed and stop and discuss the ideas in the books and reflect on our values. **ah, but shopping!** Have I failed when one of my daughter's favorite activities is spending money with me in malls? After consideration, I realized this is one of the few times we are alone together, since the males in our family hate to shop. She doesn't beg for things she doesn't need. She just likes being out and about. **being in the midst** of more than enough often gives us a chance to talk about our values. **"oh, laura,** look at this lovely sweater!" "But Mom, we don't need clothes that expensive!" "What do you think of this dress?" "Didn't you notice it needs to be dry cleaned? Why spend that kind of money?" **my children sometimes** beg for more material things. But when they think about what matters most, they want my time, to eat together, read books, or wander about. During these times we discuss our response to Jesus' call to life. *—Susan Mark Landis*

do I give the people who love me what they most want from me?

34

Books, pancake ingredients, and transportation to the mall—these can be used to create special occasions with people we love. We can use physical objects to create works of art. When we do this, we express the image of the creating, loving God within us.

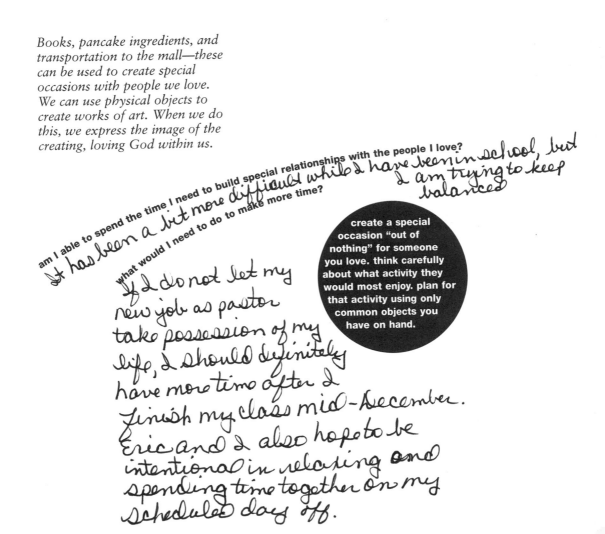

am I able to spend the time I need to build special relationships with the people I love?

what would I need to do to make more time?

create a special occasion "out of nothing" for someone you love. think carefully about what activity they would most enjoy. plan for that activity using only common objects you have on hand.

It has been a bit more difficult while I have been in school, but I am trying to keep balanced

If I do not let my new job as pastor take possession of my life, I should definitely have more time after I finish my class mid-December. Eric and I also hope to be intentional in relaxing and spending time together on my scheduled day off.

revenge of the gadgets

"Where your treasure is,
there your heart will be also."
—from Matthew 6:19-21

11

I'll **admit it,** I am a typical male gadgeteer. I had ample time in Swaziland to plan, scheme, and rationalize the purchase of gadgets while on our upcoming home leave. • Bubble-jet printer: needed for writing project. • New idiot-proof camera: needed because our other one gave out (and I am a picture idiot). • Bible software: needed to help write sermons for home leave. • Computer memory upgrade: needed to run software. • Fax modem: needed to fax this article. • Radio gadgets. **the list goes on.** I have had a buying moratorium on gadgets for the last three years while in Swaziland and now, on home leave, there was time to make up. So, armed with a credit card and three-years worth of gadget savings, I struck out on the 800-number trail. **soon the delivery person** was beating a path to our door. Box after box, invoice upon invoice came piling in. What fun! Like Christmas. **like christmas** . . . too much like Christmas. North American Christmases are notorious for their emphasis on material things—gadgets. "What to get for the man who has everything." **as I opened** my boxes and set up my new gadgets, I realized I was missing something. Like the time spent dreaming of a material Christmas, I was sacrificing human interaction for contact with my gizmos. It comes down to a choice. Either I spend time with my gadgets or I spend time with my family. **now I have** another moratorium on buying gadgets. I hope it is not too late to recover the time lost.
—Jon Rudy

do my things make me more or less fully human?

STEP OUT

Consumer culture actively blurs the line between the "first set of things" we need to sustain our lives and the "second and third set" that weigh us down and sap our energy.

United States retail analyst Victor Lebow explains, "Our enormously productive economy . . . demands that we make consumption our way of life, that we convert the buying and use of goods into rituals, that we seek our spiritual satisfaction, our ego satisfaction, in consumption. . . . We need things consumed, burned up, worn out, replaced, and discarded at an ever increasing rate." (Journal of Retailing, quoted in Vance Packard, The Waste Makers, New York: David McKay, 1960).

Seeking ultimate satisfaction from owning things can be ultimately disappointing.

work through your living space and garage, if you have one. what gadgets do you never or rarely use? donate them to your local nonprofit re-uzit shop.

some of the items could perhaps been eliminated — many of them were requirements based upon the gadgets

do I think the reasons Jon lists for buying each new gadget are valid?

what makes something designed to help me cross the line into weighing me down?

— things that take up my time while learning to use them
— my phone which makes it easier to receive information on the run yet because I am on the run I don't have time to process the info

noticing our impact

"Let the floods clap their hands;
let the hills sing together for joy at the presence of the Lord."
—from Psalm 98

12

the rain often comes down hard in mountainous eastern Kentucky where I live. The rivers and streams swell with muddy rushing water. When the water subsides, it's not difficult to see where the water level has been. Plastic grocery bags, discarded diapers and empty milk jugs dot the bank, caught among the innocent arms of trees and shrubs by the river. Old tires, soda cans, and forgotten appliances are evident beneath the cloudy water. **it hasn't always been** like this. In the region's preserved areas the water runs cold and clear over polished stones and the moss is thick and green under pines lining the banks. Areas like that used to cover eastern Kentucky—before accumulation of cheap, disposable items became a daily part of our lives. **I once took** a sculpting class in which the teacher warned us to carefully consider what we create out of the earth's raw materials. "Don't forget your sculpture may survive in this world longer than you do. Ask yourself what kind of impact your creation will have." **I carry** my teacher's warning with me when I think I need another short-lived item from the discount store. How important is it? How long will it last? Where will it end up when I'm through with it? Maybe if I can use something I already own instead of purchasing something new, the streams winding down the hillsides of eastern Kentucky can start to shine and gurgle a little more clearly.
—*Liz McGeachy*

what effect does my lifestyle have on the earth?

STEP OUT

Over 100 years ago, a British economist described the "reach" of British consumers: "the plains of North America and Russia are our [British] cornfields . . . Peru sends her silver, and the gold of South Africa and Australia flows to London; the Hindus and the Chinese grow tea for us, and our coffee, sugar, and spice plantations are all in the Indies. Spain and France are our vineyards, and the Mediterranean our fruit garden." (Stanley Jevons, The Coal Question, 1865).

In today's global economy, most of us consume items brought to us from around the world. Our garbage, including exhaust from our cars and factories, is spread around the world.

We cannot see the cost of our consumer items by looking out our front window. We must learn to see with new eyes if we are to "notice our impact."

We do a lot of recycling. Only improvement would be to compost again, but space is limited.

do an "audit" of your trash. if you find items being thrown out that could be recycled, set up a recycling system to handle them.

plant a tree.

Eric donates to Arbor Day Foundation

what, if anything, threatens the beauty and integrity of my favorite spot in nature?

what would have to happen to preserve that place for me and future generations?

Lately my favorite spot has been our backyard.

choose one fairly complex item you own—a bike, a car, a stereo. find out what elements were taken from the earth to produce it, and the effect processing them had on the earth. ask yourself: how long will I use this? what will I do with it when I am finished? consider options that would have less impact on the earth. for more information **read** Stuff: The Secret Lives of Everyday Things.

priceless gifts

"If I give away all my possessions . . .
but do not have love, I gain nothing."
—from 1 Corinthians 13

'interesting topic for this particular day which is 6 months until Christmas — the biggest gift giving day of the year

acting on my thoughts

what keeps me from giving the gift of myself more often?

i **work in** the gift-giving business. **buying gifts** can by joyful. However, in a world of too much stress, too much disposable income, and too much superficial happiness, it can become a duty or an obligation. "I spent $40 on the first grandchild's graduation, so I have to spend at least that much for this granddaughter," said a frazzled customer recently. She left ten minutes later with a gift I had in effect selected. **over the years** I have received gifts that had little or no monetary value, but meant more to me than a truckload of $40 candlesticks. An unexpected phone call from a friend concerned about my health. A recipe and note saying, "As soon as I tasted these cookies I thought of you." Gifts of life and love from my own grandmother, who drove fifty miles for piano concerts, baked butter tarts by the hundreds for every special occasion, and leaves messages on my machine to welcome me home from business trips. **what is stopping me** from an act of kindness today? Why don't my good intentions become realities more often? What is it about priorities in a world of too much that makes these simple gestures of kindness so noteworthy? **today, as I rush** through work activities designed to usher in a better world, I will listen to two kindness experts: "We can do no great things—only small things with great love" (Mother Teresa). "A kind word doesn't cost a thing" (Gertie Rice, my grandmother). **I resolve to do** one unexpected act of kindness today. In the world of enough I dare to dream of, there is

6/25/15

40

enough food and shelter to go around; there is also enough kindness, joy, hospitality, and nurturing to go around. That is something I can start to make happen now.

—Doris Daley

"What wisdom can you find that is greater than kindness?"
—Jean-Jacques Rousseau

my time is the biggest gift I can give

offers to visit people, play games, take shutins for a drive

what nonmaterial gifts could I give on various gift-giving occasions?

what was the most meaningful gift I ever received?

my husband and children

the next time you give a material gift, buy it from Ten Thousand Villages or another alternative trade organization. to find the Ten Thousand Villages store nearest you, call 717-859-8120 in the United States or 877-289-3247 in Canada or visit their website at www.tenthousand villages.org.

(WOW gifts are good)

_6/26/15_

rising higher than its source

*"We are . . . as having nothing,
and yet possessing everything."*
—from 2 Corinthians 6:1-10

a **small group** had gathered in a home in Winnipeg to talk about our lives and values, and whether we wanted to "live with enough" for thirty days. We started by sharing past experiences of living with enough. **"our years** in voluntary service and then at the seminary were the best years of our lives," one woman shared. "During voluntary service we even financed some of our expenses out of our savings. At seminary none of the students had money. We scraped by on odd jobs. We didn't have nearly as many things as we do now. But we and our children remember those as the best years of our lives." **"so maybe** 'trying enough' would bring back some of that quality of life," I ventured. **"I wouldn't** even consider 'trying enough' now," she declared. **I was puzzled.** Why wouldn't she try to recapture these "best years of her life"? **she continued,** "The years after we came home were the most painful years of our lives. Our friends and people at church were building large houses, driving new cars, and going on exotic vacations. There was no support for our desire

do my closest friends nurture my deepest commitments?

to live simply. We ended up feeling out of it, like oddballs. I will never go through that again." **we sat in silence.** I was struck both by the steely determination in her voice, and the hint of tears in her eyes. How different their lives might have been had they returned to a church and community that had nurtured their ability and commitment to live joyfully with enough. *—Dave Schrock-Shenk*

42

STEP OUT

Rooted thoughts
6/29/15

There is a popular saying, "Water cannot rise higher than its source." Similarly, the people we admire most show us by their lives the "upper and lower range" of what is acceptable and possible. They either support or discourage our attempts to live in ways that express our deepest values.

Living with enough in a culture of too much demands strong peer support.

what messages about material goods do I get from my church or faith community?

our church is more generous with their material goods than they are their time

if you are not part of a group that supports you in your deepest values, build one! find people with similar interests among your friends and church members. commit yourselves to each other and to a long-term search for a different way to live. an excellent book to use in forming a community is The Different Drum: Community-making and Peace.

do my closest friends push me toward my deepest values or make it harder to live them out?

I think they agree with my values

Most of my friends have values very similar to mine. The way my classmates feel would be foreign to them as it was for me.

WEEKLY WRAP UP

What is the most important new realization about my relationship with things that I had this week?
What about my relationship with other people?

was happy to learn about IRAs investing in micro loans

ENOUGH FOR ME ENOUGH FOR ME ENOUGH FOR ME ENOUGH FOR ME ENOUGH FOR M

lighten the pack

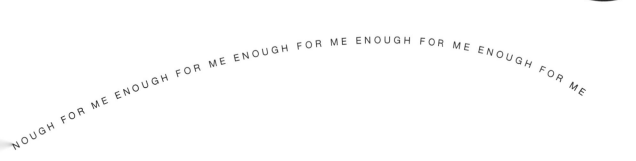

NOUGH FOR ME ENOUGH FOR ME ENOUGH FOR ME ENOUGH FOR ME ENOUGH FOR ME ENOUGH FOR ME ENOUGH FOR ME

a walk to digayap

*"Better is a handful with quiet
than two handfuls with toil, and a chasing after wind."
—from Ecclesiastes 4:4-16*

after four hours on mountain trails I get to Digayap, home of Philippine Mennonite church leaders Norma and Edwin Lorenzo. Rice farms in the valley are bathed in soft color as workers walk home along green trails to their pots of cooked rice. **Norma and Edwin's** house is made of rough boards cut from surrounding trees with corrugated tin for a roof. It seems empty when I enter. **a closer inspection** reveals a collection of simple possessions: a mat, blankets and pillows for sleeping, two or three changes of clothing for each family member, and a few simple cooking and eating utensils. All their possessions would fit in a wheelbarrow. **I have visited** many poor families in the Philippines, but this community seemed different. No "grinding poverty" here. Small plots of vegetables and fruit trees surround their house. Children appear healthy. **as we sit** in the glow of a homemade oil lamp after a supper of rice and sardines, I ask Norma and Edwin if they are happy with their lives. Except for the long distance they must travel to schools and hospitals, they say, they feel content. **we used to think** the development process would allow poor people to catch up with the rich. But ecologists tell us we would need five more earth-sized planets to provide the resources and absorb the waste if everyone lived like the average North American. **instead of solving** poverty by giving people slices of a bigger pie, we may need to change how we slice the pie we have. —*Dale Hildebrand*

could I be more content with fewer possessions?

The earth pays a heavy price for the things we use. The global economy has reached the limits set by the capacity of the earth to provide resources and absorb waste.

Robert J. Coen, a senior vice president of McCann-Erickson WorldGroup, projected global advertising at $411 billion in 1997. We receive more than 3,000 messages a day urging us to buy. Yet even if we buy something we see advertised, the advertisers will still be after us the next day for more. We're like hamsters in an exercise wheel: the harder we run, the faster the wheel spins! We can never spend our way to satisfaction.

how can I explain Lorenzo's answer that they are happy with their lives?

it is about what you do with your life

Life is more than possessions

what criteria do I use to determine what I truly need and what is nonessential?

- cost of the item
- desire

buy now!! and
— SAVE!!

carry a small notebook with you for one day. every time you notice a message urging you to buy something, jot down where you were and how you received the message. at the end of the day, determine where you get the most messages urging you to buy. for one week, limit the messages you receive from that source.

travel lightly on this earth

*"Is not life more than food,
and the body more than clothing?"*
—from Matthew 6:24-33

16

preparing for a three-year term of service in Kenya, my husband and I spent hours carefully packing. "If in doubt, leave it out," was our motto, as we proudly fit everything into three boxes, two backpacks, and various carry-ons. **almost three years later** in Kenya, we helped a young Maasai man prepare for a year in Canada as an exchange visitor. We explained Canadian customs, food, and weather. We also met at the airport to "send him off." **we found** Julius near the check-in counter. "Where is your luggage?" I asked. **"here,"** he said, gesturing to the small bag he carried. **"that's it?"** I exclaimed. "It's not even full!" **"it's enough,"** he said. **but Julius also** brought two vans, rented for the occasion, packed full of Maasai friends and relatives coming to say good-bye. Dressed in brightly colored traditional garb, they surrounded him with concern and goodwill. **this deeply moving** experience has stayed with me. A young Kenyan man, carrying fewer possessions than I would consider "enough" for a weekend trip, heading off for a year in a distant, unfamiliar country. What Julius did carry with him was far more significant—the love, support, and sense of identity embodied in the bright red, yellow, and blue-clad throng of chanting, singing, and waving fellow Maasai.
—*Deborah Fast*

what in my life gives me a sense of security?

Clothing gives our bodies privacy, and protects us from the elements. Julius had few clothes in his small bag, yet felt he had enough.

Clothes can also express our creativity and originality. Clothes can distinguish between rich and poor. Clothes can give a person a sense of belonging to a valued group.

how do my clothes reflect my personality and my values?

how do you find this out?

did the people who made my clothes get a fair wage for their work?

- most are conservative
- I try not to wear clothes that accent my full figure
- usually sensible

I have no idea, but probably not

go to your clothes closet. choose enough clothes to wear a different outfit each day of the week. put the other clothes aside. wear only the clothes you've chosen for the next two weeks.

— this is what I did during CPE and was so glad to be able to wear other outfits

6/29/15

in the palace of the poor

"This poor widow has put in more
than all those who are contributing ..."
—from Mark 12:38-44

17

Vietnamese celebrate tet, the lunar new year, by donning new clothing, visiting friends, and eating special foods. One year Ba Hein, a refugee in a camp near the town of Quang Ngai, invited us to enjoy a Tet meal with her. We reached her home late in the afternoon. **Ba Hein's** one-room bamboo and mud house was in the center of the camp. The kitchen was a lean-to in the back. **Ba Hein graciously invited** us to sit on low stools drawn up to a table. In a corner of her house I saw family photographs, including one of a young man and small child. She said they were her husband and daughter who had been killed by American artillery in the war. **Ba Hein served tea** from a pot with a broken spout. The cups were beer cans, scrubbed immaculately clean. **as we sipped** tea, Ba Hein busied herself preparing and serving the few dishes. She did not apologize for the meager fare or for the sad state of her home. She served that meal with dignity, confident her hospitality was as valuable as that of the wealthiest homes in Quang Ngai. **as we left** I turned to bid Ba Hein farewell. She stood at the door, strong and defiant, smiling confidently. I had been served a meal as though I were a king, in the palace of the poor.
—*Max Ediger*

what is required to treat someone royally?

invite someone you would "never invite to my house" for a meal.

she served the meal with dignity

what attributes of Ba Hien led Max to describe her house as a palace?

are there people in my community I would never invite into my home?

probably the homeless

have your household identify the five most important functions in the house that are done using "labor saving devices." who uses these devices most often? who would do this work if you used less energy intensive methods? what involvement by your entire household would be needed in order to make these changes?

why would I not invite them?

1. laundry
2. all water tasks
3. dishwasher
4. microwave/cooking
5. transportation

Eric + I would most likely work together

— I would feel guilty for having so much when they have nothing.

— It would make me feel vulnerable and uncomfortable.

carrying water

"The earth is the Lord's
and all that is in it."
—Psalm 24:1-6

18

my landlord employs Hari, eleven, to help with the family's household work. One of Hari's tasks is to pump water from the underground well and transport it in a bucket to the ground-level tank. From there, the water is pumped by electric motor to the roof tank. **during Nepal's dry season** I would not have water if it were not for Hari. Every time I open my water tap I think of Hari and how hard he works so that I can easily access water. I remember he is not in school and his future holds limited options. **Hari is a happy boy**—he whistles and beats his empty bucket as if it were a drum. He smiles and greets me warmly. He often comes to my door to ask for a glass of water. He likes to drink my filtered water and craves recognition. I never refuse Hari's requests for water. **water sustains** my life. Without it my body would dry up quickly and wither like a parched rose. I need water to keep my body clean and to cook my food. I need it to drink with lemons or tea. I need it to wash my clothes and flush my toilet. But when every drop is pumped and carried by Hari, I feel compelled to use as little as possible. Yes, I maintain my standard for good health and clean environment but I now use far less water than I ever have used before.

—*Catherine Mumaw*

how much water would I use each day if I had to pump or carry it by hand?

BASIC TREK

Most people in North America don't have a Hari to pump their water. But the water has to be brought into our homes somehow.

The "Hari" of North America is electricity. Electricity pumps our water, keeps our food cold then cooks it, and lights our homes. Yet while electricity is relatively cheap, there is a high cost to the earth for the power we use.

Most people in North America use electricity generated by burning fossil fuels—coal, oil, or gas. These fuels are dirty to produce, and they emit carbon dioxide (CO_2) when burned. The average Canadian needs 2.34 hectares/5.7 acres of crop or forest-land to absorb the CO_2 they produce each year. The average United States citizen needs slightly more.

install a low-flow shower head in your bathroom.

— We have already done this

if you have a standard water heater, replace it with an "on demand" or solar-thermal collector system. research the best system for your house or dormitory. find out more with the Solar Living Source Book from Real Goods Trading Corporation at www.realgoods.com or 800-762-7325.

how is electricity I use in my house generated?

I don't know, but we do have a programmable thermostat, limit electrical use when possible

cycle of breath

*"God saw everything that God had made,
and indeed, it was very good."*
—from Genesis 1

19

i bicycle to work because I like using my body first thing in the morning: stretching my legs, wind in my face, reaching deep into my muscles at the first hill, waking them up and breathing fresh morning air. I avoid the crush of sweaty people on public transportation and bad-tempered drivers on jammed-up roads. **cycling home** after a day of meetings revives my tired mind and limbs. I am reminded of the beauty of God's creation: green trees, singing birds, winding streams, and brilliant flowers. I even enjoy biking in the rain on cold days, because when I get home and peel off my clammy clothes, a steamy hot shower is waiting. **lately, I noticed** my lungs being filled with exhaust from cars and tour buses. If I cycle fast and push myself, raspy gasps for air come from my mouth. I have never had asthma. I think that might be changing. **now I wear** an air filter face mask. I prefer to keep my lungs, even if I look stupid. The mask is hot and stifling and I can no longer smell the scent of hot grass in the sun, damp earth in the morning, or azaleas in full bloom. What a dilemma: to smell the earth or preserve my lungs. **we are linked,** you and I, by the world we live in and the air we breathe.
—Reina C. Neufeldt

**what price am I
willing to pay to
swim against
the tide?**

54

"If you think cars are healthy, close your garage door and start the engine." (author unknown)
North American society is built around the private car. Yet driving a car is one of the most environmentally destructive things we can do. Every gallon of gasoline we burn in our cars releases five-and-a-half pounds of carbon dioxide, the main greenhouse gas.

If we want to substantially reduce our effect on the earth, we must get out of our cars and onto buses, trains, and bikes. Our ability to make this individual response is heavily influenced by decisions of our larger society. Supporting public transportation systems is necessary to enable all of us to shrink our ecological footprint.

the bus does not provide service to our area. they are just now starting to address sidewalks for new building project

what feelings do I have as I ride the bus or train?

figure out the number of miles you drove last year. (Canadians average 18,000 kilometers a year. people in the United States average 20,000 miles a year.) use your car's average fuel efficiency to figure out how many pounds of carbon dioxide you released into the atmosphere last year. devise a plan for getting where you need to go that would reduce your carbon dioxide emissions by 75 percent. institute those changes for one week. consider extending those changes for one month.

I would love to be able to read for pleasure during a commute

what am I able to do while riding a bus or train that I cannot do while driving a car?

There is really nothing I can do. Gives me a feeling of powerlessness.

7/2/15

growing corn

"Prosper the work of our hands!"
—from Psalm 90:13-17

20

Our study group stood in the middle of a steeply sloped cornfield near the top of a mountain in southern Mexico. We asked the farmer how much he paid the women from his village who weed the corn, and how much he paid to rent the field and the buffalo to plow it. **one tour member calculated** the cost of the inputs against the expected yield. "You could buy the same amount of corn in town for less than it costs you to grow it," he exclaimed in surprise. "Why do you bother growing it?" **the farmer paused,** startled by the question. He looked out at the view. We turned and saw anew the spectacular valley, the river running by the houses far below, the other mountains ringing the valley. We felt the breeze cooling our hot bodies. **he raised** his hands, first toward the people from his village, then toward the valley below; "To grow your own corn . . . ," he started, then stopped. "To grow your own corn," he said again, then fell silent, unable to finish an answer to a question he could not fully comprehend. Although one man spoke Spanish and the other English, it was not language that separated them, but their different views of life. **the North American** used numbers to evaluate corn as a finished product. The Mexican farmer valued the experience of growing corn for the way it maintained his relationships with people in his village, preserved the way of life handed down to him, and allowed him the physical sensation and beauty of working in his cornfield. —*Dave Schrock-Shenk*

what seems right to me

what "bottom line" do I use to decide what something is worth?

If all the food that is grown in the world each year was divided evenly among all the people in the world, and none was fed to livestock, each person would have approximately 3000 calories a day.

The majority of the people in the world are able to eat nutritious meals every day. Close to two billion farmers grow the food they and their families eat. Many of them live in societies that value the act of growing food almost as much as the food itself.

Yet almost one billion people wake up each morning without being assured of having enough food for the day. Many others struggle with problems that come from eating too much.

eat quickly, but usually sitting down — I need to learn to savor the flavors more

do I eat my food slowly and reflectively, or do I most often eat on the run?

how could I buy more of my food from farmers in my area?

market to table, coop or go to farmers markets

make a meal for your family or Trek **group using food from your immediate area. invite someone from your community who raises food to share your meal. Learn what it means to them to raise food for others. you can find international recipes in** Extending the Table, **available from Provident Bookstores, 800-759-4447.**

7/3/15

take this, it's the best i have

"Mary took a pound of costly perfume . . .
anointed Jesus' feet, and wiped them with her hair."
—from John 12:1-8

21

In 1983 I volunteered in the refugee assistance program at St. Francis Presbyterian Church in Fort Worth, Texas. One day Rodrigo approached me. **"we are grateful** for the beautiful things people have given us," he started. "But people always say, 'Take this. We don't use it anymore.' It feels like they are giving us their throwaway things. That makes us feel bad. **"in my country** I would say, 'Take this. It's the best that I have.' Even if it was very simple, we would give it to someone because we thought it was good." **"I see** what you mean," I replied. "But here it hurts peoples' pride if they need to receive gifts. So they say, 'I don't need it anymore' to try to make it easier for you to accept."

but new questions were raised in my mind. Why do we give leftovers? I had happily donated to the program several T-shirts I never wore anyway. **the next time** there was a drive for clothes, I gave away one of my best blouses. Along with the "Ouch! I'm going to miss that blouse," I tried to feel the pride of saying, "Here. Take this. It's the best that I have." **during our time** in Central America I struggled with accepting gifts from our neighbors. The only chicken is killed for us. The best chair is offered. Precious time is spent answering our questions. **their example** has become my challenge.

how can I learn to say joyfully, "here. take this. it is the best that I have"?

—Kathy Ogle

Thrift and frugality are at the core of a life of enough. These values can also be used to make ourselves rich.

One defense against a culture of individualism is to generate a spirit of generosity.

We received years of "free room and board" from our parents or other family members in our early years of life. The bountiful earth was given freely to human beings. When we give something to a person in need, we are simply passing along what we have received.

when have I most joyfully given to someone in need?

everytime I write a check for charity

what allowed me to give so joyfully?

I love to give

make a list of all the things you have received without payment from your family, friends, your society, and from God. list the things you have given for free to family members, friends, and those in need. do these lists feel "balanced" or "unbalanced"?

WEEKLY WRAP UP

Does the idea of reducing my use of things feel
more freeing or more restrictive?
Does the example of other people who are living
fulfilled lives with fewer things motivate me?

ENOUGH FOR ALL ENOUGH FOR ALL ENOUGH FOR ALL ENOUGH FOR ALL ENOUGH FOR ALL ENOUGH FOR Al

week four

**stay the
course**

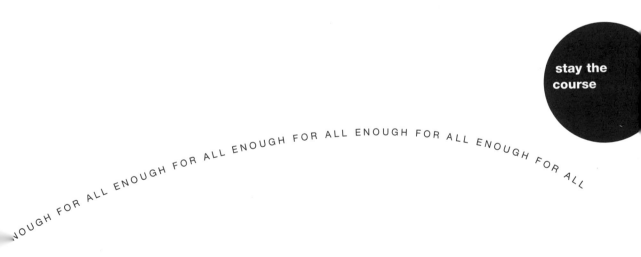

…NOUGH FOR ALL ENOUGH FOR ALL ENOUGH FOR ALL ENOUGH FOR ALL ENOUGH FOR ALL ENOUGH FOR ALL

squeezing the balloon?

"Give me neither poverty nor riches;
feed me with the food that I need."
—from Proverbs 30:7-9

22

Viola, a study tour participant from Texas, shared her story with the group that morning. **she had worked** at a Dockers pants factory in San Antonio until Levi-Straus moved the operation to Central America to get cheaper labor. Since then Viola had been working with the other laid-off workers to get the benefits Levi-Straus owed them. **later we left** to visit a maquila, a factory where Hondurans assemble products for export to the Northern Hemisphere. **as we walked** into the maquila, tour members were surprised to see a huge Dockers sign at the entrance. **during our tour,** the plant manager spoke of the benefits the maquila industry brought the hundreds of young men and women bent over their sewing machines, sewing as fast as they could to make their daily quota. **during the workers' lunch break,** Viola sat in front of a machine identical to the one she had worked on in Texas, remembering the years when she had been happy earning money to support her family. Now, a Central American woman was sitting at her sewing machine, happy to be earning money to support her family. **that evening** the group was confused as they processed the day. Viola was struggling to support her family after her layoff. Yet hundreds of Hondurans, while earning wages far below what Viola had earned, were making far more than they had ever earned anywhere else.

—*Daryl Yoder-Bontrager*

are we so interconnected with the rest of the world as to be like a balloon that puffs out on one end when it is squeezed on the other?

Enough for me is not enough!

The point of Trek *is not to make ourselves well fed, less stressed, and more happy—yet unconnected to the rest of the world. The point is to work to bring ourselves and all the world's people into that good place of enough. To do that, we need to change the systems and structures that produce both excess and need.*

Working at systemic change is hard work. Living with enough in a culture of too much is hard work. This week we will reflect on the spiritual resources for Trekking over the long haul.

create more demand/lower wages/raise prices

what would need to happen to have enough work for both Viola and the women in Honduras?

learn a different skill to find a new job.

do I know anyone who is out of work?

Hope + Jeanne

invite a person who is looking for work to a meal to talk about his or her search for work.

—Can inquire of people at MYN suppers

american meals

"He asked Jesus,
'And who is my neighbor?'"
—from Luke 10:25-37

23

my **American Airlines flight** was packed. Passengers from a canceled United Airlines flight had switched to American at the last minute. **the pilot** addressed us on the intercom: "We're glad we had enough seats for our friends from United. Unfortunately, we don't have enough meals. When the flight attendants come by, tell them if you're 'American,' in which case you'll get dinner, or 'United,' in which case you'll get a soda." **at first** I was relieved. I was an "American passenger." I would get supper. Then I thought about my seatmates. Would I share my food with them if they were "United"? **I was relieved** when my seatmates told the attendant they were also "American." But then I started wondering if the people in the seats right behind me got food, and the people behind them. Should I share my food with them? If I started sharing, where would I stop? **I didn't turn** around to check. As long as I didn't see them, I was able to eat. **I face the temptation** "not to look" at the hungry or homeless people in the world. But I know looking away makes me a bit more calloused, and a bit less human. **gaining an awareness** of those with too little—better yet sharing a meal with them—makes me more human.
—*Dave Schrock-Shenk*

what do I need to help me respond more faithfully to those in need?

64

Most people with too much never look those with too little in the eye. Even when they live in the same country, or the same city, rich and poor people seemingly live in two different worlds.

The Scripture passage for today tells of a Samaritan who responded with compassion to a person he met by chance along the road. The question, "Who is my neighbor?" can also refer to the people we see everyday when we look out our front window.

Every Wednesday night Sunday—pretty much anytime I am at church

when, if ever, do I come face to face with poor people? how does that happen?

what values and beliefs are reflected by where I choose to live?

we chose to live where we do because of the school system (Windsor Woods) and then we moved to a neighborhood with bigger houses because we wanted more space

find a map of the city, county, or municipality in which you live. with your Trek group, identify the "rich neighborhoods" and the "poor neighborhoods." research the history of the poor neighborhoods. were they always that way? how are separate rich and poor neighborhoods created? mark the places you and your group members live. how does everyone feel about living where they do?

7/6/15

tears of the poor

"Just as you did it to one of the least of these . . . you did it to me."
—from Matthew 25:31-40

24

the poverty all around us in Vietnam at times convicts us of our relative wealth. It can also become commonplace. **Mrs. Ly,** a farmer from the rural North, has showed me how insulated from poor people's needs and feelings I can become. **on New Year's Day** Mrs. Ly and Mrs. Ngoc, a fellow farmer, brought gifts of rice, mung beans, and fruit to our office in Hanoi. As we chatted a beggar stopped at the gate. We remained seated, almost not registering her presence. But Mrs. Ly and Mrs. Ngoc immediately got to their feet, reaching into their pockets for money to give. They, who have so little even compared to the Vietnamese people who cook and clean for us, let alone us rich foreigners, were the first and only ones to respond, to give without a second thought. **Mrs. Ly had personally** experienced some of the hardships this person with the outstretched hands was facing. Her response was one of understanding and compassion. **as church workers** we seek to be a presence where life is difficult. However, we need people to be present with us as we try to overcome our insulating wealth and privilege to live out Jesus' teachings. We need people like Mrs. Ly to help us connect with poor people whom Jesus calls us to love. No matter how big or small our store of riches, we can give joyfully, freely, and in overflowing measure.

what sense of connection with people in need can unlock my compassion and generosity?

—*Betsy Headrick McCrae*

was there *not really* ever a time when I really didn't have enough money?

how did or does this make make me feel about people who are wealthier than me?

do I have a personal relationship with anyone who is struggling to afford the bare necessities? *fellow students*

what does my relationship with them add to my understanding of life? *reinforces how blessed I've been*

— I also try to bless them

spend an evening talking with someone who experienced financial hardship at some point in his or her life. what were the low points of that time? what was good about his or her life at that point?

7/7/15

enough solidarity

*"We have nothing here but five loaves and two fish. . . .
All ate and were filled."*
—*from Matthew 14:13-21*

25

during my three years of service in Kinshasa, Zaire, I witnessed the absolute poverty and suffering of many close friends. While I tried to respond, I often found myself saying, "It's never enough." **with my volunteer salary** of $50 a month, I was often utterly overwhelmed. The few dollars or bag of rice I could give felt like a drop in the bucket. Even if I helped a few, the needs were endless. "It's never enough." **I began to** question why God would bring me here to witness this overwhelming suffering without giving me the resources I needed to respond. **eventually** I came to understand how Zairians were surviving. They called it African Solidarity. When you have a little bit, you share. When you're in need, you ask friends and family for help. Everyone gives as they are able, because no one is sure when they will need to ask. **a wonderful sense** of community is built when every person contributes as they are able. Now it seems egotistical to think I could or should take on the burdens of the world. I know God brought me here with limited means to participate and suffer with others, as one of many in God's family. I give as I can, and help those in need think how they can share in their turn. **if we act together** in solidarity with others, there can be enough. —*Krista-Anne Rigalo*

do I miss the chance to do what I can because I can't do it all?

When people enter into relationships with each other, every part of their life becomes part of the relationship: their joys, their needs, their dreams and goals, their triumphs, and their failures.

When we define another person solely on the basis of that person's needs, it it a sign of an incomplete relationship. It leads to a desire to "fix" that person's needs and move on to another relationship.

In mature relationships, there are times and seasons of giving and receiving, and of learning to appreciate what each person contributes to the other.

identify the problem in the world that is the most overwhelming to you personally. identify an organization that is addressing that particular problem. what is one change you have made during Basic Trek **that saved you money? commit to continuing that change for one year and send a check once a month for the amount you save to that agency. if your choice freed up time, consider volunteering for that agency.**

am I reluctant to contribute toward a need my gift cannot completely meet?

what could I do to be able to give more to meet the needs of those who do not have enough?

I like to do my part in hope that others will participate as well

encourage Eric than we have enough and that we can give more so that others can have enough as well

7/8/15

stuck at the high end of the scale

"You are not under law
but under grace."
—from Romans 6:5-14

I can really identify with this

26

dear sisters and brothers working on "World of Enough," I'm flattered that you invited me to write a meditation for your reflection guide. I live with too much. I wrestle with how to live on less, sometimes willing to work harder than other times. **our family's use** of gas alone probably means we'll never get to the "living lightly" class. But I feel clearly that God has called us to these jobs and this community, where absolutely nothing is within walking/biking distance and no public transit exists! **many of us** are basically good people caught in a system not of our own creation or preference. Unlike our sisters and brothers caught in the unfair system at the other end of the resource-use scale, we benefit rather than are hurt by the system. But we also need compassion as we try to change a system we didn't create and sometimes seem unable to escape. **I want to work** toward a more sustainable lifestyle. It will be painful, and I'll experience some guilt along the way. But if I want to make changes that will last the rest of my life, I need to see hope and possibility, not yet another heavy and unbearable burden.

how can I work for just enough without tying myself into knots of guilt and despair?

—*Susan Mark Landis*

Dear Susan,

Like you, my wife, Carolyn, and I have tried to simplify our lives, yet we remain overconsumers. I don't know how to move to a sustainable lifestyle. Yes, I know what to do—take the bus instead of the car, eat beans instead of meat, and have more people share our house. But I don't have the necessary spiritual resources, the creativity and drive, to actually get there.

You and I know some of the negative consequences of how we live. We know we can't shame ourselves out of this way of living. We also know too many poorer brothers and sisters around the world to be able to say, "It's too hard. Why bother?"

It's quite a dilemma to be a rich Christian in today's world! Yet I believe the gospel holds the promise of liberation from our wealth. We need to work together to claim that promise. "World of Enough" is about finding other people who help us shape a model of enough in our own context. Then we live with enough for thirty days. We discover that it is both possible and fun.

You and I both want concrete handles on what enough is. We will find and shape those handles as we search together.

Yours in peace, David Schrock-Shenk

how do these letters speak to issues I face in my own life?
I understand perfectly

write a letter to the organizers of Basic Trek. tell them the challenges you face as you attempt to move toward enough. tell them your dreams—how you want to live. tell them what you need to continue to move toward enough. send your letter to Communications Dept, MCC, PO Box 500, Akron, PA 17501, USA.

a vision for the church

"I will pour out my spirit on all flesh;
your sons and your daughters shall prophecy. . . ."
—from Joel 2:23-29

27

et us proclaim a vision for people of faith, inspired by the teachings of Jesus. **Christians have declared** the year 2000 the Year of Jubilee! Christians all over the world have canceled all debts, pooled their money, and divided it up so people everywhere have what they need to live. **churches from** the so-called third world have sent workers to the United States and Canada to teach us how to travel without needing cars and airplanes, how to cook simple, nutritious food, and how to have fun without spending money. **all over** the Western world, Christians have drastically reduced their incomes and have moved in together, creating contemplative, active communities. Tax collectors come to find out why so many people no longer owe military taxes. **freed from the weight** of their former possessions, their souls are expanding and their spirits soaring! Compassion, peacemaking, and joy are endemic among them. **the Holy Spirit** is breaking through even such institutions as racism, class distinctions, and patriarchy. Unchurched people are flocking to their fellowships, eager to share in the life of Christ. **the creative power** of God, the compassion and joy of the Holy Spirit, and the unconditional love of Jesus are pouring out upon people everywhere. **this revolution** was begun by Jesus, who, being fully human and fully God, came to teach us to be like him, and to invite us to receive the power to do so.

what is my vision for the church?

—Nancy Brubaker

72

Christian faith calls us to go beyond our own resources to respond to the needs of the world. We gain strength for the long-term work of living out our faith by keeping the vision of God's will for God's people before us.

write on paper what you think would be happening in the world if all God's children were living according to God's will. share your vision with your Trek group. discuss how you can work together to start making your visions a reality.

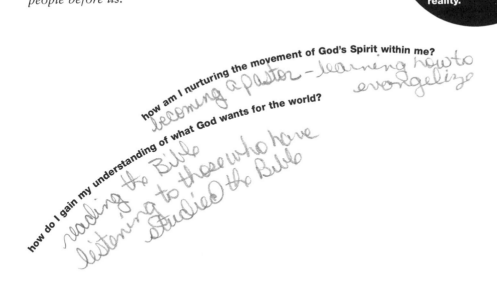

how am I nurturing the movement of God's Spirit within me?
becoming a pastor — learning how to evangelize

how do I gain my understanding of what God wants for the world?
reading the Bible
listening to those who have studied the Bible

upside-down praying

"The one who had much did not have too much,
and the one who had little did not have too little."
—*from 2 Corinthians 8:8-15*

28

"**G**od, please help** the poor get rich
and the rich get poor
so they know what it feels like.

"And then, God,
let everyone switch back to medium
and let everyone have the same amount of food and money. Amen."

this was Ben's prayer at supper. Ben has lived all his seven years with us in service assignments. He's probably spent a fair bit of time mulling over the meaning of "enough." **when we lived** in a Zairian diamond-mining village, Ben spent a lot of time with two different playmates. **Rupert was British,** the only child of a diamond specialist. Rupert seemed to possess every toy that could be airlifted into the interior. Sabu was a child of refugees burned out of their home in another region of Zaire. On the days his mother washed his only set of clothes, Sabu had to stay in the house. **Ben had great times** with both friends, although hardly ever as a threesome. He drove remote control cars and experimented on the electronic keyboard at Rupert's house. He molded miniature mud bricks and chased chickens with Sabu. Ben switched back and forth between economic extremes with apparent ease. **Ben did not pray** that all the poor people would be rich. He prayed that all people could be medium. Somehow Ben sensed the freedom of enough.

—*Jeanne Zimmerly Jantzi*

do I think a world where everyone has enough is part of God's vision for humankind?

At the end of Trek *we review the path we traveled these twenty-eight days.*

what did I learn about "enough" during Trek**?**

keep on trekking.

We also face the future.

can we experience "enough" as a gift throughout our lives?

Today's Scripture calls Christians to the place of "enough," where no one has "too little" or "too much." Trek suggests many of us need to reduce our material consumption by two-thirds to reach "enough." Others may have different ideas of how to get to "enough."

Yet all are called to reflect on the "liberating paradox of biblical proportion" contained in Anthony de Mello's story of the fisherman.

Might embracing "enough" free us from the stress and dissatisfaction of trying to get "as many things as possible"? Would using only our fair share of the earth's resources mean there will be enough for others? Do we need to actively work with others so they can experience the health and joy God intends for all?

How can we give our children a world that has enough for them, and their children?

Our paths will take us in different directions. "Enough" will look different for each of us.

May we trust in the God who created us all to guide us on the way. May our journey to a World of Enough, at times long and difficult, be blessed with joy.

APPENDIX I

ecological footprints

human beings use the earth's resources to meet their physical needs. The earth provides resources and absorbs our waste. Croplands and oceans produce food. We get coal, oil, and other fuel from energy land. Forests produce paper products and absorb carbon dioxide resulting from fossil fuel usage. Roads and buildings are the final use of degraded land.

It is possible to add up the total amount of land required to supply an individual's needs—this can be referred to as a person's "Ecological Footprint."*

The ecological systems on which we depend are naturally self-renewing. Schools of fish replenish themselves. Forests reseed themselves. Groundwater is renewed by the rain. Forests grow by absorbing carbon dioxide and giving off oxygen. We can use these systems in ways that allow them to regularly renew themselves. Humans and all living creatures can live sustainably on the earth.

But we can also put so much stress on these natural systems that they can no longer function as they should nor renew themselves adequately. The stress we put on the earth depends both on how we meet our needs, and on how much we use. Advanced technology makes it easier to use resources, and almost inevitably leads people to use more. People who use advanced technology almost always have a larger Ecological Footprint than those who use less technology.

This is not a value judgment. People do not have a large Ecological Footprint because they are "bad people," but because of decisions they make about how to build their houses, get to work, eat and clothe themselves. They make these decisions based more on what society tells them is necessary than on an understanding of how their decisions will affect the earth.

average North American ecological footprint

Ecological Footprints for a country are calculated by totaling the resources used by the total population, figuring out the amount of land needed to produce those resources, then dividing that land by the number of people living in that area.

The average Canadian's Ecological Footprint is almost 4.3 hectares(ha)/10.6 acres, roughly the area of three city blocks (see chart on next page). The Ecological Footprint of the average United States citizen is 5.1 ha/12.6 acres, somewhat larger. People in the United States can use the categories in the chart as a fairly reliable guide to their consumption patterns.

None of us get the resources we need nor get rid of our waste in the area right outside our doorsteps, or even in our local area. The fuel for our cars, for instance, is often drilled and refined in countries far from where we live. Our car exhaust goes into the atmosphere and is carried by the wind across provincial, state, and even national lines.

Those of us in industrialized countries reach into ecosystems outside our own borders to get our resources and dump our waste. For instance Lower Fraser Valley in British Columbia has approximately 4,000 square kilometers and 1,800,000 people. Assuming the average Canadian consumption patterns, this regional population has an Ecological Footprint of 73,000 square kilometers. The people in this region use an area 19 times larger than their home territory to support their lifestyle.

U.S. average footprint in acres per person (Numbers may not add due to rounding; Information courtesy of Redefining Progress.)

	ENERGY LAND	CROP LAND	PASTURE	FOREST	BUILT AREA	SEA	TOTAL
food	2.0	3.1	2.4	0.0	0.0	0.1	**7.7**
household	3.7	0.0	0.0	1.4	1.2	0.0	**6.4**
transportation	5.8	0.0	0.0	0.0	0.8	0.0	**6.7**
goods	4.3	0.2	0.1	1.1	0.1	0.0	**5.9**
services	2.3	0.0	0.0	0.7	0.1	0.0	**3.1**
other	0.1	0.0	0.0	0.0	0.0	0.0	**0.1**
TOTAL	**18.3**	**3.4**	**2.5**	**3.2**	**2.3**	**0.1**	**29.9**

fair share ecological footprint

The fact that people in one country use resources from other countries is not a problem by itself. Even people in poor countries use resources from other places. The problem is that wealthy societies can extend their Ecological Footprints far into the rest of the world. But they cannot create more land. Their oversize footprint represents an "ecological deficit" with the rest of the world.

We can determine each person's "fair share" of the earth's resources by dividing the 7.4 billion ha/18.2 billion acres of ecologically productive land in the world by the 5.8 billion people on earth. Each person potentially has 1.5 ha/3.7 acres available to meet her or his needs.

According to the chart on the following page, people in India need to consume more to get to their fair share. Do the people in Canada and the United States need to consume less or can we just "expand the pie"?

Humans are currently using 4.8 billion ha/11.85 billion acres of land for crop lands and pastures. A forested area of 1.7 billion ha/4.1 billion acres is needed to supply our wood in a sustainable manner. It takes 3.0 billion ha/7.4 billion acres to absorb the excess carbon dioxide released by our fossil fuel consumption. This total of 9.6 billion ha/23.7 billion acres is more than the 7.4 billion ha/18.2 billion acres that is currently available to be used!

How is it possible to use more land than is available? We do that by using forests, soil, and air in ways that make them lose their ability to regenerate, and make them unavailable for future generations. In economic terms, we are using (natural) capital to finance current consumption.

Since we cannot make the earth grow, we must meet everyone's needs while actually shrinking our current overall consumption!

average personal consumption comparison

	USA	CANADA	INDIA	WORLD
average footprint	30 acres	20 acres	3 acres	7 acres
CO_2 emissions	20 tons/yr	15.7 tons/yr	0.9 tons/yr	3.9 tons/yr
freshwater withdrawal	1,688 m³/yr	1,431 m³/yr	497 m³/yr	—
paper consumption	335 kg/yr	225 kg/yr	5 kg/yr	51 kg/yr

Information courtesy of Redefining Progress and additional sources:
CO_2 emissions: 1996 data from International Energy Agency, CO_2 Emissions from Fuel Combustion, 2000 Edition.
Freshwater withdrawal: 2000 estimates from The World's Water 2000-2001, Peter Gleick, Island Press, Washington, D.C., p. 205, Table 2.
Paper consumption: 1997 data from Paper Cuts: Recovering the Paper Landscape, Worldwatch Paper #149, Janet Abramovitz and Ashley Mattoon, p. 13, Figure 2.

one fair share model

If we want to preserve the earth, and if we want there to be "enough" for all God's children, those of us with oversized Ecological Footprints must use fewer resources and produce less waste.

We can live the joyful, fulfilled lives God meant for us using our fair share of the earth's resources. To get there, most of us need to use one-third the amount we currently use. Put another way, we need to reduce our emission of carbon dioxide, use of fossil fuels, paper consumption, and use of fresh water by about 75 percent. How could a person live like that in North America? There are many ways to reach that target. Here is one model.

The "fair share person" lives with others in a house with about 250 square feet of living space per person. The insulation in their house exceeds "government requirements" by 50 percent. The household uses a solar hot water heater, which makes its Ecological Footprint for heating water more than 100 times smaller than heating water with fossil fuel! The house most likely shares walls with other houses, increasing its fuel efficiency even further.

This fair share household shares their morning paper with another. They read their magazines at the public library. They drive no more than 6,000 kilometers/3,720 miles a year in their car. The train ride to visit family members in other states and provinces becomes a special part of each year's vacation. A fair share person rides her bicycle to work. On cold days she takes the bus or carpools.

Each summer this household plants a large garden. They use mainly fertilizer from their compost pile. Their canning and freezing parties become family and social events. They buy the food they can't grow from local farmers and co-ops. They save their use of food shipped from far away for special occasions. Birthdays and anniversaries are celebrated by getting together for meals using recipes from around the world. Gifts are homemade or bought in fair-trade shops.

The relatively small budget of fair share families means many parents can work half-time outside the home. They spend the rest of their time helping their children with schoolwork, playing with their children, volunteering in their neighborhood, working in their garden, reading books, and serving on church committees.

global classes

a key concept of *Basic Trek* is the idea that there are three global socioeconomic classes. There are no neat lines between the classes. People at the top of the Destitute class and at the bottom of the Sustainer class are not very far apart. But in general terms, broad markers divide the human family in three groups.

overconsumers The global consumer class is roughly equal to the number of destitute. Their diets contain a large amount of meat, processed and packaged food, and soft drinks. Most of their food travels long distances to the places where they buy it, and is packaged in disposable packaging. Their houses are large, heated, and often air-conditioned. They almost always contain refrigerators, clothes washers and dryers, water heaters, microwave ovens, televisions, VCRs, and telephones. They may have many personal electrical appliances, such as hair dryers and curlers, computers, can openers, and clocks. They usually travel in private cars. When they use public transportation, they usually use airplanes. This group, one-fifth of the human family, earns 64 percent of total global income. This is thirty-two times as much as the poorest fifth.

Many people in the United States and Canada think of themselves as either middle class or even relatively poor in relation to the "super wealthy" people in their own societies. Yet almost anyone who lives above the official poverty line in these two countries is in the global upper class.

sustainers People in the global middle class eat diets based on grain, with occasional meat. They usually have access to clean water. They live in solid but not large houses. They have access to electricity, and have home appliances ranging from lights, radios, televisions, refrigerators, and washing machines. They travel by bus, bicycle, or train. Collectively, they earn 33 percent of total global income.

destitute People who are destitute eat grains, root crops, and beans. They rarely have access to clean water. They live in houses constructed of scrap wood, tin, or branches. They travel by foot or sometimes on animal transportation. Collectively, this group forms one-fifth of the global family, but earns just 2 percent of global income.

This idea is more fully developed in *The Consumer Society and the Future of the Earth* by Alan Durning, W. W. Norton, 1992.

APPENDIX III
additional resources

B O O K S

parent trek From the creators of *Basic Trek* comes a resource to help you raise children to be more creative, generous, peaceloving, and joyful in today's society. "Each chapter is short enough for busy parents to read easily, yet crammed with insight" (Andrea Brown, mother and pastor). *By Jeanne Zimmerly Jantzi. Herald Press, 2001.*

consumer's guide to effective environmental choices Practical advice from the Union of Concerned Scientists. Contends that rather than looking at across-the-board consumption reduction, people should focus on the lifestyle changes that affect the environment most. *By Michael Brower and Warren Leon. Three Rivers Press, 1999.*

earthkeepers Offers environmental perspectives on hunger, poverty, and injustice. Explores root causes of environmental degradation, and a biblical theology for caring for the earth. *By Art and Jocele Meyer. Herald Press, 1991.*

extending the table: a world community cookbook You don't have to leave home to experience a wide variety of foods from other countries and learn about other cultures. Interspersed among taste-tempting recipes are stories about how hospitality is practiced around the world. *By Joetta Handrich Schlabach. Herald Press, 1991.*

for the common good An economist and a theologian write a compelling, understandable explanation of why a sustainable world requires a new economic base. The best background book available. *By Herman E. Daly and John B. Comm Jr. Beacon Press, 1994.*

material world: a global family portrait Families around the world emptied their houses of all their worldly possessions for these snapshots. Beautiful and moving, it illustrates the reality of the three global classes. **women in the material world** using a similar format focuses on the material circumstances of women. *By Peter Menzel. Random House, 1995.*

more-with-less cookbook A favorite of many families. Full of recipes and suggestions on how to eat better and consume less of the world's limited food resources. A classic that has not only changed how people eat, but their entire approach to life with the more-with-less philosophy. *By Doris Janzen Longacre. Herald Press, 1976.*

the poverty of affluence Points out the impossibility of ever satisfying a need for things. Urges community and non-material pursuits to find satisfaction instead. *By Paul L. Wachtel. New Society Publishers, 1989.*

simpler living compassionate life This attractive and readable book contains essays and reflections by prominent Christian thinkers and activists. It goes beyond "doing with less" to "living more." *By Michael Schut, ed. Living the Good News, 1999.*

solar living source book Excellent source of data and background information for those who want to live sustainably. Also sells many appliances. *By John Schaeffer. Real Goods Trading Corporation, 1994.*

state of the world Annual report on how the natural systems of the world are faring. Contains some alarming statistics, as well as careful prescriptions for how to achieve balance with the earth. *By Lester R. Brown. W. W. Norton, published yearly.*

stuff: the secret lives of everyday things From our morning cup of Colombian coffee to our South Korean-made sneakers, it traces the environmental impact of the consumer decisions most of us make every day without thinking. *By John C. Ryan and Alan Thein Durning. Northwest Environment Watch, 1997.*

'tis a gift to be simple Explores the "why" of a simple life by telling the story of a family who successfully adopted a simple lifestyle. *By Barbara DeGrote-Sorensen and David Allen Sorensen. Augsburg Fortress Press, 1992.*

VIDEOS

affluenza Explores the epidemic of shopping, overwork, stress, and debt that is infecting Americans in record numbers. Traces the historic roots, explores the marketing that sustains it, and offers concrete advise to find a cure. *Produced by PBS, 1997 and 1998.*

the lorax A Dr. Seuss fable for children about how people destroy the environment by only using things once. Enjoyable and thought-provoking. *Produced by DePatie Freleng Productions, 1972.*

the mouse's tale An animated cartoon that explores international food production and its relationship to hunger. A well-fed cat is confronted by his "conscience" (a mouse) as he reads in a newspaper about cats starving in Africa. **the richest dog in the world** is a sequel to this video. *Produced by Australian Catholic Relief, 1985 and 1989.*

running out of time Explores the social impact of time pressure and overwork on North American society, how much activity people fit into their busy lives, and how little leisure time remains. Compares conditions in other countries and at other times and examines solutions to overwork. *Produced by Films for the Humanities, 1994.*

All videos are available for loan from MCC.
U.S. 888-563-4676   Canada 888-622-6337

O R G A N I Z A T I O N S

alternatives for simple living Their mission is "to equip people of faith to challenge consumerism, live justly, and celebrate responsibly." They offer an extensive list of resources for celebrating seasonal events such as Christmas, Lent, and Easter, and special events such as weddings. Some resources available in Spanish. *phone 800-821-6153 www.simpleliving.org*

center for the new american dream National nonprofit organization dedicated to helping people change the way they consume to improve quality of life, protect the environment, and promote social justice. Their motto: "More fun, less stuff!" *phone 301-891-3683 www.newdream.org*

mennonite environmental task force Promotes awareness among Mennonite constituents and church organizations of how Christian commitment encompasses concern for God's creation. *phone 316-283-5100 www2.southwind.net/~gcmc/etf.html*

new road map foundation Practical tools and innovative approaches for mastering and managing basic life challenges. Known as the source of the best-selling book *Your Money or Your Life*, they traditionally focused on health, personal finances, and human relations. *www.newroadmap.org*

rocky mountain institute Entrepreneurial nonprofit organization that fosters efficient and restorative use of resources to create a more secure, prosperous, and life-sustaining world. They provide resources that help corporations, communities, individuals, and governments protect and enhance natural and human capital, largely by doing what they do far more efficiently. *phone 970-927-3851 www.rmi.org*

about the editor

Dave Schrock-Shenk served as MCC co-country representative in the Philippines from 1985-89. From 1989-2000 he worked as the Global Education Coordinator for Mennonite Central Committee in Akron, Pa. He currently lives in Goshen, Ind., with his family, where he continues to work on global education projects.

Mennonite Central Committee (MCC) is a relief, service, and peace agency of the North American Mennonite and Brethren in Christ churches. MCC has some 1,500 workers serving in fifty countries in food production, health, education, job creation, refugee assistance and peacemaking.

21 S 12th St, PO Box 500, Akron, PA 17501 USA; (717) 859-1151 or toll free (888) 563-4676
134 Plaza Dr, Winnipeg, MB R3T 5K9 CANADA; (204) 261-6381 or toll free (888) 622-6337
www.mcc.org